FEELINGS:

EXPLORING INNER SPACE

Feelings:

Exploring Inner Space

by

Jeffrey Schrank

PAULIST PRESS
New York / Paramus / Toronto

Library of Congress
Catalog Card Number: 73-75742

ISBN 0-8091-1772-X

Cover and Text Photos by
Charles Gatewood

Published by Paulist Press
Editorial Office: 1865 Broadway, N.Y., N.Y. 10023
Business Office: 400 Sette Drive, Paramus, N.J. 07652

Printed and bound in the
United States of America

Contents

**I.
Tricks
of a Self—
Escape
Artist**

High in the Catalina Mountains
Earl Francis claimed an abandoned gold mine.
1964
Earl was an amateur painter who liked quiet.
"A man can be free in the mountains," he said.
No bosses or time clocks.
No road scarred his isolated mountain
overlooking eerie, empty stretches
of Arizona desert.
He built a house,
alone.
One year later his house was finished.
Then the government spoke.
"You're trespassing on Federal land."
Federal law allows a home to be built
on a mining claim,
Earl said.
But the mine must be productive, he was told.
Earl's mine had little gold—empty, abandoned.
The house had to go and so did Earl.
The picture windows, fireplace,
the porch, rock-lined walkway—
they all had to go,
and the paintings too.
So Earl walked his shaggy dog
to the house of a friend
and went back to the mountain.
It was sunset.

He sat on a keg of dynamite next to his mine.
Lit the fuse.
Not much was ever found of Earl.
His last painting survived.
One word and a large question mark:
LIFE?

Earl Francis may have acted with drama and finality, but he had the same urges as you or I. Everybody escapes somehow, withdraws, steps back and sits out a round or two of the game, of the day, or of life. From the daydream to the closed door, from the cigarette to self-caused insanity, humans take time out from playing the world game.

Life is a rhythm of engagement and withdrawal. The need to escape is as important as the need to be involved. Wanting to get away from parents, brothers and sisters, school, or the usual surroundings and routine is normal, in fact a sign of health. But for some people escape becomes a way of life. There is little engagement, little involvement and much escape. Life for such people becomes a constant search for new ways to escape.

The ultimate form of escape is suicide; it also is the fourth leading cause of death among American teenagers. Among people in their twenties in the U.S. the suicide rate has more than doubled in the past decade. Shootings and muggings make gory newspaper headlines that readers devour with their morning coffee or evening martini. But few realize that, as Pogo said, "We have met the enemy and they are we." A person is three times as likely to commit suicide as to be murdered by someone else.

A recent survey revealed that 80% of those questioned admitted to "toying" with the idea of suicide at some time in their life. Very likely many of the other 20% have simply never admitted the feelings. Suicide is the eleventh leading cause of death in this country and might rank as high as fifth if accurately reported. The temptation to self-destruct is one which occurs to everyone at some time. For suicide is the trick that would seem to magically enable escape from the one force that can never be avoided—oneself.

In a sense, suicide is a contagious disease. For when we read of a suicide or especially if we know someone who attempts or commits suicide, we are brought face to face with the question of our own life and death. In the panic of 1929 thousands committed suicide, each planting the idea in the minds of others. In Japan a young girl committed suicide by jumping into the crater of a volcano and was followed within a year by three hundred other young people. The Golden Gate Bridge and the Empire State Building are favorites for suicides, and when Marilyn Monroe committed suicide in 1962 the suicide rate in Chicago and New York in the following days rose to five times the usual average.

Sigmund Freud proposed that each person has a "death wish" that occasionally surfaces. Life is insecure and dangerous while death is sure and peaceful. His guess seems backed by a culture which thrives on high speed life styles, risk-filled driving, dangerous sports, toxic drugs, a nuclear arms race and frequent wars. It is even possible to view two armies poised on a battlefield as an attempted mass suicide.

How many automobile "accidents" in which a car

suddenly loses control and slams into a tree are really a moment of giving in to the temptation to self-destruct? In how many people who die of a natural illness is death speeded or even "caused" by a giving in to the desire to escape?

If a narrow footbridge were placed one foot above a field it would be deserted, except maybe for the local pre-school kids who would turn it into a playground. But if that same bridge were placed over a canyon thousands of feet deep, the curious would flock to it from all over the world. When tourists are precariously balanced on the bridge, they realize they are only one step from potential death. Perhaps this is why they have come, to entertain that temptation, to defy death. The fear of heights might be a disguised voice of the struggle that goes on within each person. That queasy feeling, that weakness when looking down from fifty stories up, that thumping of the heart as you slowly drive by a fresh auto accident, that exhilaration on a roller coaster has something to do with life, death and escape.

Although every suicide is an attempted escape from what is considered the confinement of life, not every escape is suicidal. Escape is often a sign of common sense and the recognition of the needs of the human personality. Assuming you have your own favorite escapes, you can learn quite a bit about yourself by observing what you avoid. Learning about yourself by watching what you withdraw from is not easy; many people were taught that escape is always a sign of weakness so they find it difficult to face their own escapes. Awareness of how you "escape" and what you escape from takes time and practice. In this chapter we'll take a look at three common forms of escape: receiving compliments, I-less speech patterns, and dreams.

The most basic escape in our culture is also the most frustrating and impossible: escape from self. In a sense, this desire to escape from self is a form of what could be called "self-wipeout." Self-escape is a way of saying, "I'm not here," or "I'm bad and no good," or "I don't exist." There is no question that you engage in some of this self-escape and that it stunts your psychological growth.

One symptom of "self-wipeout" is the difficulty in accepting praise and compliments. For example, Dennis was an excellent basketball player. But whenever anyone told him what a fine game he played he would either blush and look away or start a conversation about all the mistakes he made, the shots he missed and the fouls he committed. By denying himself the pleasure of praise he turned off a valuable source of self-affirmation. In general Dennis spent a lot of time thinking about his mistakes and seemed almost determined to erect a wall against praise, compliments and nice things people had to say about him. His mother was the same way. She was an excellent cook, but whenever anyone told her how good she was, she would toss off a phrase like "The oven did it," or "It was really nothing." Neither Dennis nor his mother was really humble or shy, although some friends described them as "unassuming" or "modest."

In effect they were denying themselves the nourishment of the praise that others provided. Some of Dennis' friends found that complimenting him was useless, so they stopped, thus confirming his fears that he really was no good.

Think about how you react when praised or complimented. Is it a source of embarrassment? Try to imagine or remember how you would feel if you were singled out for praise in a class or even at an assembly of the whole school. How do you feel when your relatives come up with the inevitable "My, how you've grown" or "Aren't you a big boy (girl) now!" How much praise do you toss aside with a laugh or giggle? How do you respond to compliments?

In general, if you tend to brush off praise or even hide from it, you are taking part in a subtle form of self-escape. Surprisingly many people think of themselves in terms of "I'm not O.K." and so they reject the messages that contradict this self-image; they reject the "You're O.K." messages. Why anyone would want to escape from his own goodness is hard to understand, but such running away is extremely common.

A psychologically healthy person is able to drink in praise and to soak in its warmth. For this person praise is like the warm sun after a long winter. He isn't always out to get praise, but when it comes he enjoys the warm feeling it gives and makes others feel good about praising him. He doesn't negate praise with "It's nothing" or "It was just luck."

Next time someone compliments you, try telling him how good it makes you feel, how thankful you are for the praise. If you can learn to do this naturally, compliments will cease to be a point of embarrassment and will become a way of affirming yourself even more. It will also help you to be able to honestly compliment others. So watch your own reactions when giving and receiving praise and see what you can learn from them.

A second symptom of this psychological rubbing out of oneself is found in day-to-day speech patterns of most people. I call this symptom "I-less" speech. In order to detect this kind of speech in yourself you will have to practice self-awareness until you can hear yourself using it. Once you become aware of how often you escape from yourself in ordinary conversation, you can take some action to restore yourself.

Here's a bit of a conversation taken from cafeteria talk at a high school. See if you can detect this self-escape taking place. Don't be too surprised if you see nothing unusual about the conversation.

(1st girl)   What did you do Saturday?
(2nd girl)   Well, you know how sometimes you just want to get out of the house?
(1st girl)   Yeah?
(2nd girl)   Well, Jan and I went downtown shopping and *McCabe and Mrs. Miller* was at the shopping center. It was really a dumb movie, a big drag. In fact it got so bad we just left about halfway and went to get a pizza.

Perhaps you noticed that the first girl verbally wiped herself out in that little exchange. She was talking about herself, yet, except for one time, she avoided using "I." She used words like "you" and "it" when she plainly meant "I." When she said, "You know how sometimes you just want to get out of the house?" she wasn't really asking the other girl a question; she was saying, "I just wanted to get out of the house." When she said, "It was really a dumb movie, a big drag," she wasn't talking about the movie as much as she was making a statement about herself, saying, "I was bored" or "uninvolved."

Notice the difference. Saying "It was a drag" blames the movie and puts the feeling of boredom out there somewhere. It is a denial of a simple feeling. There is a feeling-difference between saying "It was boring" and "I was bored." "It" is a thing-word; "I" is a self-word.

This example is not significant in itself, but if this kind of speech is a general pattern, as it is with many people, then there is significance. In other words, if a person generally replaces "I" in speech with substitutes such as "it" or "you," that person is verbally wiping himself or herself out of the remark, and this denial of self can become a permanent part of a much larger pattern of self-escape.

Right now you might still be saying, "I don't see why such a common speech pattern makes any difference." Try observing your own speech and that of others. Catch yourself wiping out that "I" and try restoring the "I." The experiment will make you aware of your patterns of avoiding responsibility for your actions. Restoring "I" will also enable your communication to be more direct, honest and self-full.

Here are a few self-elimination statements you can practice with. Take each one and change it into an honest statement which restores the "I":

1. "You just can't get ahead in this class."
2. "Mr. Rovers really got people angry today."
3. "It was really an exciting book."
4. "It dropped out of my hand."
5. "The bus went off without me."
6. "It's really a tear jerker."
7. "People are afraid to even walk the dog at night in our neighborhood."

8. "That dress looks great on you."
9. (Passenger in speeding car) "Do you have to drive so fast?"
10. (Person who has said little in group discussion remarking to a talkative person next to him) "You talk too much."

(Some correct answers are suggested on pages 13-14.)

Try to notice in these examples how the statement feels different when the "I" is restored. Notice that we are not saying that "you" or "it" should never be used, nor are we saying that anytime a person uses "it" or "you" he is showing signs of verbal suicide. We are looking for regular, habitual speech patterns that might reveal subtle attempts to escape responsibility for some feeling. It is understandable that in our culture people regularly attempt to escape responsibility for feelings, for feelings are not really encouraged. And showing or even admitting feelings in public is likewise discouraged.

This escape from "I" in ordinary speech is only a symptom of what could potentially become a more serious problem—total self-escape. Such attempted self-escape can come through drugs, suicide, insanity or even an obsession with work. Drug addiction and insanity aren't simply misfortunes which "happen" to people; they are chosen by individuals in flight from themselves as a way to hide from a troubled self.

By noticing how you participate in the great escape, you can learn what it is you avoid and what causes conflict. In your experiment with avoiding "I" in speech, you might have noticed a pattern, a certain situation in which you avoid affirming yourself. With the knowledge of this behavior pattern you might be able to solve some inner conflict or at least be more aware of it.

Oftentimes the simple awareness of a trait previously hidden changes the situation.

A third common way of escape is to daydream. In school young people are taught that daydreaming is a distraction, a waste of time or a bad habit. Actually it is a valuable and relatively safe escape which can provide some self-knowledge. Be aware of when you daydream and what you "dream" about. For example, if you find that you daydream a lot during history classes, you might realize that the history class is a situation from which you would like to escape. Probably no great self-revelation there. But if you continue to be aware of your daydreams, you might find some rather surprising patterns that will reveal a previously hidden desire to escape.

The content of daydreams is even more useful. If you regularly find yourself lost in far away thoughts about yourself as ravishingly beautiful or ferociously masculine, that is likely a sign that you are somewhat dissatisfied with the way you appear. Or you might consistently daydream of being rich, yet claim that making a lot of money isn't really important. The daydream never lies and is probably more revealing of your real desires. Those who have been jilted daydream of revenge; those who feel like a nobody daydream of world fame. The fantasy in a daydream is usually the reverse of a present frustration and thereby an accurate and never-lying indicator of our frustrations and needs.

So rather than a bad habit, daydreams are a way of escaping that have great potential for developing increased self-awareness. For example, if you dream about being in love with a famous singing star, you might not need that particular superstar but it would indicate that you would probably like to get to know that guy or girl down the block who you think is so attractive. If you daydream about being an actor or actress or writer, it might very well indicate that you have some talent in this direction that is worth developing. The reality might not be as glamorous as the dream, but the daydreams never lie; they come to the mind uncensored and so they deserve a careful listening. Examine the content of your daydreams to see what unfulfilled wishes they contain.

Dreams while sleeping are another valuable, never-lying form of escape. Studies show that everyone dreams every night. If you say, "I rarely dream," what you mean is: "I rarely remember my dreams." Try to recall dreams. Keep paper and pen near the bed so that you can write them down as soon as you wake up. Give yourself suggestions before you fall asleep to remember your dreams. Try to remember the dreams in as much detail as possible.

We spend about one-third of our short lifetimes in the state of dreaming. To throw away all this time by simply "forgetting" dreams is to throw away a vital part of our experience. Dreams don't have universal meanings; there can be no dictionary of dream interpretations, but they can tell you things about yourself. Whatever you dream is part of yourself, often a part of yourself that you keep "asleep" during the day, a part that you hide, repress or refuse to admit.

Learning from dreams takes practice and teaching —a skill beyond the scope of this book. But one simple observation to make about your dreams is to realize what you avoid in dreaming. For example you might dream of falling but always wake up before you reach the bottom. Or you might dream of killing someone or of being killed, but wake up just before you do so.

What you avoid in your dreams is a good indicator of what you fail to face while you are awake. Fantasize and relive the dream and let it go past where you stopped it before. When awake, try to relive the dreams like instant replay. Fall all the way, go into that cave, be killed or kill, and see what comes next. You might learn something about this, even if it is only that you fear the dark, death, or your own destructive impulses. Dreams will not help you predict the future, but they might give you valuable clues to the present.

Self-escape comes in many disguises, from dreams, innocent blushes and quiet fears to tragedy and suicide. No one has yet succeeded in escaping from self, but each person in each generation nevertheless tries. Some simply become frustrated and deceive themselves, but a few learn from their escapes so that they are no longer driven by the need to escape.

Confronting oneself honestly is an activity that our society seems to fear. In Battle Creek, Michigan a justice of the peace decided that Americans fear confronting themselves more than losing money. So he forced traffic violators to sit alone in totally empty rooms for three to five hours. The townspeople were enraged and demanded that the judge stop the punishment on the grounds that it was unnecessarily cruel.

Maybe the judge had the right idea. He took away the props from the self-escape artists. Maybe the punishment really was to make self-escape impossible, and that involves too much honesty for comfort.

Possible Rephrasings of
Self-Elimination Statements (See page 10)

1. "I can't seem to get ahead." "I'm frustrated."
2. "I was furious with Mr. Rovers."

3. "The book really excited me."
4. "I dropped it."
5. "I missed the bus."
6. "I really cried when I read it."
7. "I'm afraid to go out in our neighborhood at night."
8. "You look nice."
9. "I'm scared!" or "Slow down!"
10. "I can't get a word in edgewise."

2.
The Tightly Wound Modern Man and His Portable Tension Traps

MILWAUKEE (AP) — A man strolled through a bus and handed a $10 bill to each startled passenger before vanishing out the rear door.

By the time police caught up with the 55-year-old man Thursday, he had given away an estimated $1,400 to strangers and was on his way back to a savings and loan association to withdraw $2,000 more.

Police persuaded officials at the firm not to allow their generous customer to withdraw more from his account.

Police Capt. Jerome A. Jagmin said the man, whom authorities declined to identify, was taken to a hospital after it was reported he was despondent over the death of his wife two months ago.

The man explained that he had only wanted to brighten the Christmas season for others, Jagmin said.

Perhaps the moral of the story is that anyone crazy enough to give away money must be ill. No one questions the sanity of bank robbers, but to give money away . . . ?

The man was very likely acting for his own health. His stress and sense of loss after the death of his wife had to be dealt with somehow. For some people, despondency would result in suicide, ulcers, lack of appetite, a loss of interest in life, or even a lifetime drinking spree. For this man the stress of the loss of his wife led

16

to his going out to others. A doctor could hardly have prescribed better medicine.

The man somehow knew that when under stress some kind of action is needed as a relief. Without releasing action, stress and tension can build up until it leads to what we call a nervous breakdown.

Actually, there is no such thing as a nervous breakdown. Nerves don't break down. The expression "nervous breakdown" is used to label a multitude of problems that almost always involve an inability to cope with day-to-day living. Another common misconception is that outside forces and pressures build up and cause a person to fall apart. In reality, people are not broken down by forces from outside; rather they break themselves down. A person who "breaks down" escapes responsibility for his actions and at least temporarily solves his problems.

Not only are these dramatic breakdowns self-caused; so are the ordinary day-to-day tensions and nervousness. Both are states which a person inflicts upon himself. No one can *make* you tense or nervous except you. Tension works from the inside out, not outside in.

Taking a closer look at tension and nervousness, we see that they have little to do with those mysterious but marvelous things we call nerves. For simplicity and accuracy, consider nervousness as a form of fear or preparedness to face a difficult situation. You might recall "stage fright" before speaking in public, playing a sport before an audience, or giving a class report. You might also have noticed that once the activity begins the fear often disappears. I know of at least one professional football player who arrived before each game hours early and spent most of that time throwing up everything he had eaten in the past twenty-four hours. He was a veteran player, yet this was his ordinary way of preparing for a game. Once the game began he was fine and usually played well.

Businessmen often find themselves in fearful situations where they can take no action and feel a need to release this energy on workouts, punching bags, golf, or even in yelling at their wives, dogs and children. Of course it would be both healthier and more effective if that energy could be applied to whatever is causing the fear instead of a substitute.

Let's take a look at a typical case of tension. Picture yourself in your English class. You receive a note saying you are to report immediately to the principal's office. You have no idea why you are called and the note gives no hints. Try to imagine how you would react both in mind and body. What would you think when you received the note and how would you feel? Mentally walk out of the classroom, down the halls to the principal's office, walk through the door and announce your presence to the secretary or whoever is there. Then wait ten minutes, sitting on a metal chair against the wall until the principal comes and says that you may enter.

Some commonly reported and observed reactions to this situation include sweaty hands and a general increase in perspiration, "butterflies" in the stomach, a feeling of blood rushing to the head especially when the note is read and the principal appears, a general body tightness and often an increase in the pitch of the normal speaking voice. People in this situation most often used words such as "nervous," "tense," or "scared" to describe how they felt. Many claimed they were comfortable, yet showed all the signs of nervousness, while others avoided describing what they felt by using words like "funny," "curious" or simply "nothing."

If you examine this situation and others in which you personally felt nervous you will probably find that a common factor is the presence of fear and certain physical reactions.

Fear is best described as the body preparing itself for either an attack or a defense against an attack. Fear is a cornered cat arching its back, a panther tensing to pounce, or a human walking down a street at night and spinning with muscles tight and fists clenched at the sound of running footsteps approaching from the rear.

Fear and stress cause people to perspire easily, especially under their arms and in the palms of their hands. Sweat is the body's cooling system. When the body senses a situation that will require some action, the cooling system automatically turns on even if the action is never taken. A person who cannot perspire at all would actually be in danger of overheating. People find this nervous perspiration a minor problem but it is part of the system of communication within the body. Listening to this body talk can tell you a lot about what you feel in any given situation.

Fear is not in the head; it's in the body. This is true of any feeling. Given the proper instruments, scientists can actually measure fear by the chemical and physical changes in the body. When certain changes take place, we say "Im scared."

Fright is a valuable emotion for self-protection. But when a condition of fear becomes constant and normal, we begin to describe a person as nervous, tense or, more recently, "uptight." The word "uptight" is a perceptive one, since a tightening of the muscles is among the most common symptoms of fear. Like a cat forever cornered, the uptight person is in a constant state of tension, prepared for any attack from what he views as a hostile environment in which he lives. Tensing muscles is a way of preparing them for action, to run, duck, kick or strike. If the muscles are tensed but the tightness never released, the flow of blood to the body and freedom of movement are seriously reduced. This excess tension, repressed energy, makes a person dis-eased. He becomes an individual who finds the flow of feelings blocked by the tension. The uptight person is a scared person.

To get some idea of how the uptight person feels, tense as many muscles as you can right now. If you are alone, try standing up and walking a few steps, then whirling around prepared to face a mugger three steps behind you. As you turn prepared to attack or defend, you are tense. Without loosening your muscles, try to act out affection, sadness or hurt. It's nearly impossible. The nervous, tense person, like a cat with a permanently arched back, is never able to curl up to relax or be soft.

Re-laxing simply means to make muscles lax again. If they have become permanently tensed, great effort is needed to re-lax them. What often happens is that tense people, over a period of years, lose the ability to relax. They often resort to drugs such as alcohol, nicotine, or even sedatives and tranquilizers to achieve chemical relaxation. True, these chemicals do relax muscles temporarily, but once worn off the person goes back to his unconscious habit of muscle tensing and is unable to understand why relaxing is so difficult.

In a rare moment of honesty the tense person might admit to a close friend: "My job is getting to me," or

"My wife and kids just get on my nerves." The tragedy here is that the person blames the tension on others instead of himself or herself. A change in jobs or a divorce is a logical outcome of such thinking, but when the situation has changed the tense person will find that he has brought his portable tension machine with him into the new situation. His real enemy is himself, a foe that defies escape.

A man earning a living is almost required to be uptight in order to survive in the business world. He grows his own portable bubble that he carries around to keep people from getting too close. Closeness might hurt. He is an efficient worker and perhaps a highly successful money earner. He's so busy earning money he's forgotten how to live.

In this world feelings are normally hidden by tensing muscles, and ulcers and nervous breakdowns are common. The businessman wears clothes which reflect his uptightness; he ties a piece of cloth around his throat, puts a strap around his waist often tightly, binds his feet in hard leather with string or metal buckles, and works completely cut off from nature. The working woman often dresses even more uncomfortably in an effort to appear attractive. It is little wonder that such dress and environment for eight hours a day for years constitutes a challenge to the survival of a person's humanity.

The inhabitant of the "working world" has learned that in order to survive he must wear a mask, insulate himself, become encrusted and invulnerable. He makes himself "uptight" as a twentieth-century version of medieval armor to protect himself in his daily battles. But sometimes the mask becomes permanent; the armor is never taken off and family and friends wonder why the change. The price he must pay for this armor of tension is a decrease in feelings which give joy and pleasure and satisfaction. Learning to tense muscles and hide feelings is a skill which is nearly impossible to turn on and off between work and family life.

Even headaches are self-caused by tensing frontalis muscles inside the head for long periods of time. People who understand tension can actually learn to "cure" their own headaches without using drugs. In any self-caused illness, aspirin or pain-killers don't make you feel *better;* they make you feel *less.*

One result of permanent tenseness is that it diminishes feelings "across the board." It not only lessens feeling pain, but also joy. Muscular tension is a form of armor to protect against uncomfortable feelings. Perhaps uptightness is needed as a defense against what is viewed as a cruel world. Or maybe people who make weapons of war or who have abundant wealth amid poverty or who spend eight hours a day in utter boredom have to be "uptight" so that they can live with themselves without too much pain.

So the problem is not to eliminate tension or fear. They are far too valuable as survival mechanisms to wipe out. The problem is to avoid unconscious but more or less permanent tension which prevents the enjoyment of life. This permanent tension is not a rare occurrence; it is present to some extent in every person. For a middle-aged adult already caught in the tension trap, this is an extremely difficult process that might require drastic changes in life style. For most people under twenty-one, however, there are a few simple (but not easy) steps to take to avoid the tension trap.

On a physical level tension is caused by the absence of movement and oxygen, and their lack causes more tension in a vicious circle arrangement. In general, feelings of any kind are strongly influenced by breathing and movement. When a body part is seldom moved and receives insufficient oxygen, it loses its feeling. The most common example of this is when your leg or arm "goes to sleep" as might happen if you sleep on your arm, thus cutting off both movement and circulation of oxygen-carrying blood. If this happens you will notice the eerie sensation of having an arm completely without feeling. It might scare you a bit as you restore oxygen and movement to bring it back to life.

The arm "asleep" is an extreme example of what happens to the whole person if breathing and movement are restricted. Try an experiment right now. Lie on the floor and put your hands on your chest for a minute and simply breathe normally. Be aware of how your chest moves as you breathe. Then move your hands down to your stomach, just below your navel, for a minute and feel your breath. Don't breathe any more deeply than normal.

Most people are shallow breathers, limiting their breath to the chest and not using the lower part of the trunk of the body. In your experiment you can detect shallow breathing by noting how much of your body a breath travels through. If only your chest moves, you're a shallow breather. Shallow breathing reduces the supply of oxygen and impedes the flow of feelings. Shallow breathers thus contribute to their own tension. An animal relaxing is a fine human model. Notice how breath moves like a wave in an animal, from the chest almost the length of the body; this is natural breathing. Breathing restricted to the chest causes tension and makes relaxation difficult.

In addition to breathing shallowly you very likely

limit the oxygen supply when you need it most by holding your breath in situations of stress. The lack of oxygen causes more fear and anxiety which causes you to hold your breath more and the vicious cycle has struck again. With some practice and self-awareness you can catch yourself unconsciously holding your breath.

The reason for the breath-holding is to minimize pain, whether real or imagined. For example, when the dentist's drill bites into your tooth you almost instinctively hold your breath. Or, if you witness an accident or see a fight, you will very likely find yourself holding your breath. With self-observation you might find that you add to your own tension by holding your breath while driving, taking tests, arguing, or simply talking to someone you fear.

Have you noticed the sigh of relief after taking a difficult test? The sigh comes from a resumption of normal breathing, held during the test. Of course the very act of holding your breath while taking a test makes the flow of oxygen to the brain more limited and therefore hurts thinking. The fact that you can't think like you usually can causes more tension and the vicious circle might very likely result in poor test results. The circle can be broken by simply stopping and taking a good deep breath (inhale and exhale) and then breathing at least normally for the rest of the test. Don't be afraid to try a few deep breaths even if the room is quiet. With increased awareness of your breathing habits you can probably find dozens of times when you create your own tension by failing to breathe properly.

Ever notice how many people light up a cigarette when in a tense situation, saying they "need" a smoke?

Taken objectively, this might seem a strange habit, for the active ingredient in tobacco is a drug, nicotine. Nicotine is a stimulant that increases heart beat, stimulates the flow of adrenalin, and raises blood pressure. It has no ability whatsoever to calm a person down, and its only use outside of smoking is in insect sprays. What does calm a person down in smoking is not the nicotine, but the extra air he inhales with every puff. Cigarettes have a calming effect in spite of the tobacco, not because of it. Much the same effect can be achieved by proper breathing.

Tension can be discharged through movement and breathing. Of course, there is more to tenseness than this. Most tension is probably caused by imagined rather than real fears. To solve the problem of tension would include solving the problem of false fears, of the person who views the world as an enemy battleground and others as potential adversaries.

The important thing to remember is that tension and "nerves" are self-caused conditions. They are means of intra-body communication and deserve a listening rather than a cold shoulder. But as in any communication system, if the messages become constant, then the information channels become clogged up and other messages cannot get through. If tension and nervousness are appreciated as a means of providing information and if they are released rather than resisted, they become psychological friends rather than enemies.

3.
**The Art
of
Anger**

Anger is a basic human emotion that demands expression. Those who expect you to "never get angry" or to "always play it cool" are asking the impossible. If you believe anger to be an irrational and destructive emotion, you will probably make regular attempts to conceal your anger; you might even succeed in convincing yourself that you never get angry. But these efforts and self-delusions will be far more harmful than the anger itself. Anger can be redirected but never made non-existent. People who talk about repressing or stopping anger are talking about the impossible; what they really mean is distorting anger into something else. Anger cannot be completely turned off for long periods of time without disastrous effects.

This doesn't mean that everyone should go around like a hot-head, popping off at the slightest provocation. But it does mean that in a healthy emotional climate anger will sometimes be present. Where there is no anger shown, perhaps there is not enough freedom to express the anger. This is as true for a classroom as for a household. A husband and wife who claim they never become angry with each other are putting someone on or are unaware of how they distort their anger. In fact, a test for "true love" (if such a test were possible) would wisely include a test of ability to express anger. If a person does not feel free enough to be angry with someone else, he or she is not likely free enough to love that person either.

All people become angry, although they express the anger differently according to personality. Some will explode, others simmer, others nibble away or kick themselves. But there are obstacles to the natural expression of anger in our society. In fact, we can say that expressing anger creatively is a sort of neglected art. One of the most basic obstacles to anger is a very limited and dangerous idea about "self-control."

When most people talk about self-control, they seem to mean self-paralysis: the ability to pretend that they have no feelings, that they are "cool." Learning emotional "control" is a goal given to children as they become adults. But a more useful and sane approach is to teach the art of emotional expression. If people can learn to express emotions honestly and accurately, control will be no problem.

The assumption behind this distorted idea of self-control seems to be that lurking underneath the surface of each person is the terrible urge to go berserk or commit murder. In other words, those who stress control over expression don't really trust or believe in people. They very likely don't even trust themselves. A person who is angry is no more "out of control" than a person breathing heavily after running three blocks.

When people talk about "controlling" feelings, they seem to mean "repressing" the feelings. They are like a bad driver who would try to "control" his car by using only the brakes. The driver with such an approach would not only cause accidents and have a difficult time getting anywhere, but he would eventually cause his car to break down. So it is with people; there are controls other than emotional brakes, although brakes are helpful and sometimes urgently needed.

Besides the obsession with "self control," another obstacle to the expression of anger is the tendency of some people to want everyone to love them and their fear that anger will cause people to dislike them. These people play the role of the "nice guy" who doesn't make waves, keeps everyone happy and never gets angry. His role playing is probably an attempt to gain love from people, but he would never admit to being a love-starved child.

A third block to expressing anger is the currently popular respect shown for the "cool" person, the individual who never "blows his cool" in any circumstance. This seems only a slightly new twist on the old idea of the self-reliant pioneer able to withstand harsh winters, death, attacks from Indians, starvation and gun battles without a sign of emotion. Cool means cold, and cold means lacking in warmth and feelings. What "being cool" comes down to is the old American taboo against showing feelings in public, a taboo that results only in dishonesty and frustration.

Being angry usually shows caring. If you don't care about something or someone, you don't become angry —apathetic perhaps, but not passionately involved in anger. The cool person thus would give away the fact that he was concerned, that he cared if he was angry. And caring is too close to affection for comfort.

Perhaps you see yourself in one of these blocks to anger and are asking: "What happens to anger that is not expressed?" It is converted, to borrow Dr. Theodore Rubin's phrase, into a "slush fund" that hinders the development and health of the individual. It can turn into anxiety or a lasting depression, lingering guilt, extreme over- or under-eating, escape through sleep, or the inability to sleep. Unexpressed anger can be turned into oneself in the form of various disguised forms of self-sabotage such as negative remarks about oneself, use of drugs, or frequent accidents.

The person who attacks himself instead of expressing anger at someone "out there" is at least sure that his anger will strike his mark. Turning anger inward takes away much of the risk. I can easily berate myself and tell myself how dumb and no good I am and not have to worry about being attacked in return. A simple example of anger turned inward is the person who stubs his toe against a box and then mentally kicks himself for being so clumsy; thus his pain comes in a double dose.

Dammed-up anger can turn into an actual physical illness such as an ulcer or high blood pressure or a consistent stiff neck or sore muscles, or it can be turned indiscriminately outward onto some vague national phenomenon like Communism, hippies, the government, society, the police or strangers. In other words, the failure to freely express anger results in its manifestation in ways that are not effective or psychologically healthful. There is no question as to whether or not you should feel angry; the only question is how you will express that anger.

The first step in relearning the art of anger is to get in touch with your own anger, especially if you are the kind of person who believes he has anger for none. Physically the feeling of anger is signaled by an increased rate of breathing, faster heart beat, some muscle contraction, and probably a "hot" feeling which comes from the movement of blood.

Many people have been taught so well that anger is not permissable that they have actually lost touch with their anger. In a situation where anger arises in them they manage to stay cool, but they might mope or be depressed for days afterward and never make a connection between the depression and the self-deception in failing to express their anger. A person cannot be free until he has learned to accept his own anger. This means realizing that anger is a sign of health and not an uncontrollable passion or a beast within to be chained.

There are some obvious advantages to showing anger when honestly felt. But our society isn't yet ready to allow people to express anger whenever they feel it, or any other feeling for that matter. So some control is needed. One advantage of honestly expressed anger is that it is short-lived. Anger unexpressed can last days, even a lifetime. Anger admits the possibility of forgiving and forgetting. Anger clears the air, since there is no doubt how you feel, and it brings problems out into the open where they can be honestly faced.

But doesn't anger lead people to do irrational things? On the contrary. People kill and hurt others regularly out of distorted and misplaced anger rather than out of a genuine expression of anger. What this common misconception fails to account for is the difference between anger and hatred or hostility. Anger is a basic biological expression of feelings, whereas hatred or hostility is a knocking down or devaluing of another person.

For example, if one of my friends unexcusedly doesn't show up when he's supposed to meet me and I'm left waiting, I might get angry and let him know I am angry when and if he does arrive. But if I can't admit my anger, I might decide (unconsciously) to express hostility instead of anger toward him.

In the first case I would say something such as:

"I'm really mad that I had to stand here in the cold for a half hour." In hatred I would put down or devalue the other person and say something like: "Why can't you ever be on time?" or "You're really dirty to do a thing like that."

The first is an expression of honest anger and the second a form of revenge or hostility. The hostility here is likely one of being angry at your friend for making you angry, and thereby creating a feeling you cannot cope with. All this anger is then distorted into hatred. Hatred is often an attempt to make the other person responsible for whatever caused your anger; it is another form of escape from self and from your own feelings. You can learn quite a bit about yourself if you can be aware of what makes you angry and the kinds of people toward whom you feel hostility.

For example, think of the word or phrase that can make you the most angry if someone uses it on you in rage. A boy who becomes hostile when called "queer" can learn from his own reaction that he is afraid of the label and might be very uncertain about his masculinity. Names you are called that make you most angry are signs of what can hurt you most. Others who know you seem to know this and will not call you names in hatred that they think will not hurt. If being called a "fat slob" hurts, it is a fair indication that you don't like your own body shape. If you did like your shape (or if you weigh ninety-five pounds soaking wet), the phrase "fat slob" wouldn't hurt. The same applies to what you think is the worst thing you can call someone else. Very likely what you consider so terrible is something that is also a weak point in yourself.

In anger you are asserting yourself and declaring your own feelings to be valid and important. In hostility or hatred you are being aggressive and attacking the other person. Hostile people attack others in an attempt to defend and build themselves up. The fact that hostility doesn't build them up leads to even more hostility, and a vicious circle leads to an "angry young man" pattern. A hateful person is blocked from his own anger.

If we perceive another person as weak, there is a great temptation to use that person to build up ourselves. For example, you are sitting and reading a good book and along comes your little six year old sister who wants you to see her new doll clothes. Let' assume that seeing her new clothes is the last thing in the world you want to do; you're tired and simply want to sit and read. But your sister, not getting the idea, keeps pestering you. The honest approach would be to say with feeling, "I'm tired and don't want to be bothered." You could even show anger if that's how you feel. The tempting but dishonest way is to try something like, "Go take your dumb dolls and jump in the dishwasher." You've devalued her and probably hurt her. You might feel good because you hurt her, since you experienced a power within yourself to hurt. But you weren't honest and you made communication in the future with your sister just a little more difficult. If you have parents whom you feel you can't talk to, dishonesty with feelings, especially anger, might be a partial cause of the problem. An honest show of hurt or anger is often the first step in reopening blocked channels of communication.

A wrong impression you could have made from this chapter so far is that the "hot head" is the person who is most healthy and in touch with his anger. The person with a "temper" is not necessarily a person who is honest with his anger. First of all there really is no such thing as a "temper," and red hair has nothing to do with it. The word "temper" comes from the same root as "temperature" and simply indicates heat—a hot head. And remember that one of the bodily reactions that is part of anger is a feeling of heat. So a person with a "temper" is simply someone who shows anger or hostility a lot. Many times such people harbor an unexpressed anger for their parents or husband or wife and simply take it out in sports (starting fights, yelling at referees, etc.) or by getting "hot and bothered" over little things that happen.

One way to spot a temper as a dishonest way of dealing with anger is to notice under what conditions the temper is shown. If the temper flares in a way that is far out of proportion to the incident that provokes it, the temper is very likely distorted anger. For example, if someone accidentally bumps the "hot head" as he's carrying popcorn back to his girl at the movie house and he starts to shout and challenges the other person to a fight, you know that he's not merely expressing honest anger.

The fact that the person with a "temper" consistently expresses his anger at those toward whom he doesn't feel much real anger frustrates him even more and pushes him deeper into tantrums and depression.

Another common mistake is to use anger to hide hurt. Given a choice between expressing one of these two feelings—anger and hurt—most people, even the timid, would gladly choose anger. Hurt is an extremely difficult emotion to express openly. Once again we are taught that expressing hurt is a sign of weakness, and we are afraid to show our weakness since we fear it would make us vulnerable to further hurt.

The most common way to hide hurt is to cover it with anger. It's much easier to say "That really makes me mad" than "That hurts a lot." If you can watch yourself very closely, you might be able to notice that just before you feel anger or hostility you feel hurt. Many people have hidden hurt so habitually that they hardly feel it anymore; they have built up thick defenses against being hurt. Of course, the only problem with keeping out hurt is that the same screen or mask that keeps hurt away also keeps away love and affection and tenderness. I would be willing to guess that maybe eighty percent of the anger expressed in daily life is really used to cover hurt.

Sometime when you're with friends, catch yourself covering hurt with anger and try saying honestly: "That hurt." You might be surprised at what the honesty accomplishes.

Somewhere beneath all the masks and defenses, between the hot head and the cool guy, lies the honest approach to anger—an approach that is difficult to learn but one that each person has to struggle to find for himself.

Monday morning in Kobe, Japan.
Yasuhide Ikeda, age 24
driving to work on the highway.
The morning warm,
the drive relaxing.
Left arm resting on open car window.
A truck passes in the opposite direction.
One mile down the road
Yasuhide notices
his arm is missing
from the shoulder down.
He drives to the hospital.
Little blood,
little pain,
clean cut.
Hospital reports
fair condition.
Ten minutes later
police report finding an
arm
on the highway.

An amputation can take place without your knowledge. There are two ways this can happen. If the cut
is quick and clean, there is almost no pain. This is
what happened to Yasuhide Ikeda, but it is extremely
rare. The other way is for the loss to take place so
slowly that you don't notice it, like water carving a

canyon. This is taking place constantly, probably even today. What is being amputated is not an arm or leg but eyes, ears, nose, taste and touch. They are being amputated unsuspectingly by a culture which does not value or educate senses. They are being amputated by a society that reads best sellers on how to be a sensuous man or woman. They're being amputated by a society that could learn more from cats and babies than from best sellers.

Cats and babies: humans seem to enjoy both. Perhaps part of the enjoyment comes from the fact that we admire the ability of both a cat and a baby to be relaxed, playful, unworried, contented and simple. The way a cat curls up and purrs to sleep and the way a baby smiles and coos might reflect talents that adults had at one time but regretfully and accidentally lost in the process of growing up.

A Zen "parable" tells of a disciple who asked a Zen master, "What is the Tao?" (The Tao means the way or the truth.) The master replied simply, "When I am hungry, I eat. When tired, I sleep." The disciple was understandably puzzled and asked, "Isn't this what everybody does?" The master replied, "No, most people are never completely in what they are doing. When eating, they may be absent-mindedly preoccupied with a thousand different fantasies. When sleeping, they are not sleeping." He could have added that most Westerners eat and sleep when the clock tells them to rather than when they are hungry or tired.

The Zen master was telling his pupil that open senses and awareness of the present are a key to a life well lived. For us, senses also act as censors. We see, hear, taste, smell what we have been taught is correct or appropriate to sense. This phenomenon is called perceptual filtering. A New York psychologist devised an ingenious experiment to demonstrate perceptual filtering—a binocular-like device that showed a different picture to each eye. The image presented to one eye was a baseball player, while the other was presented with a bullfighter. Mexican and American school teachers were asked to look into the device and tell what they saw. A high percentage of the Americans reported "seeing" a baseball player, while an equally overwhelming majority of the Mexicans said they "saw" a bullfighter. In effect, the subjects in the experiment saw what they had been culturally conditioned to see.

Another example of perceptual filtering is shown in the French film *The Wild Child*. The film tells the story of a boy abandoned in the woods as an infant and discovered for the first time by humans at around the age of twelve. The boy had raised himself, lived in the wilds and had no contact with civilization. At first the doctors who studied him believed him to be deaf. A door was slammed behind the boy and he gave no indication of having heard it, yet there seemed to be nothing wrong with his ears. Finally the doctors noticed that he could hear certain sounds, those that he had learned in the woods. The boy was able to hear the faint sounds of wind changing direction in the tree tops, but was unable to hear a door slamming. He too heard only what he had taught himself to hear, only what his normal environment presented. So it is with every person. We never see or hear (or touch, taste or smell) things as *they* are; we always perceive reality as *we* are.

The cat and the baby, unlike the human teen or adult, never "grew up" and learned what was appropriate. They are very much in touch with their bodies and what their senses tell them. They still enjoy not only hearing and sight but the neglected senses of smell, taste and touch. They are sensuous creatures and are easily totally involved in sense experiences. Nobody seems to be as able to relax as well as a cat, few gourmets equal the delight of a baby smearing food all over himself, few people enjoy the sense of touch as much as a slinking cat, and rare are the adults who can laugh with the simplicity and delight of an infant. Judging from book titles, our culture seems to have confused sensuality with sexuality, two related but very different factors.

We still retain the expression non-sense to mean something that doesn't seem right. So people who are non-sense, who have amputated senses, aren't quite right. There is a lot of themselves that is hidden and a lot of the world that is not enjoyed. The ultimate effect of being nonsensical or not sensual is an over-all loss of touch with the world (alienation) and a loss of touch with oneself (loss of identity). The skill of being sensual has almost nothing to do with the media's ideal of being sexual; rather it is a skill so fundamental that without its cultivation an entire civilization could destroy itself through non-sense.

Smell

Smell is one of the most primitive and powerful senses man has. When man began walking upright, his nose moved further from the ground, and since he could smell the earth less, he gradually began the long and still continuing loss of the sense of smell. Compared to primitive man, modern man practically is noseless; he has changed his nose from a source of information and pleasure into one which supports eyeglasses, is picked in private, and helps in breathing.

People who live with pollution (and that would include most Americans) might find it advantageous to have less than a keen sense of smell. A primitive man in a big city for the first time might find the smells that the city dweller no longer notices more striking than automobiles and skyscrapers.

Scientists of osmics (the science of smell) claim that the potential of man's sense of smell is such that with a little training he could outsmell any hunting dog. With a highly developed sense of smell (trained in special schools) the professional sniffer would detect a world neglected by those around him. He could help police, as one police dog in the U.S. already does, by learning to smell protegestrone, a hormone left on any object touched by a pregnant woman. He would also be able to analyze mental illness. Some scientists now believe that certain mental illness, like schizophrenia, can actually be detected in body odors. If you consider this all futuristic dreaming, know that there are wine sniffers today who, by the smell of wine, can tell the kind of grapes used, in which vineyard they were grown, and even when they were picked. Even today in primitive societies, how a person smells is as important as appearance in the selection of a marriage partner. Such heightened sense of smell might even result in a few new expressions. As you leave your friend, you might be heard to say "Smell you later" instead of "See you later." It's simply a matter of culture and learning.

Judging from TV commercials, we seem to be hard at work eliminating natural odors with deodorants and creating artificial odors with heavy scents such as house sprays, incense, and perfumes. Somewhere along the line of history we decided that body smells are definitely bad. Not all cultures believe that; in fact Americans are viewed by most foreigners as having nearly an obsession with avoiding smells.

The whole world of smell is difficult to appreciate with out psychological clothespin pinching the sense of smell. Yet smell is the potential source of profound joy and has a powerful ability to bring to mind past events. Part of relearning how to enjoy smell involves simply acquiring a greater awareness of what you do smell and an open mind as well as an open nose.

Touch

There is nothing worse than being out of touch, nothing worse than living in the world wrapped up like a mummy, insulated and safe from the feel of the earth.

Any sense that goes unused deadens and withers away. Like a leg that is not walked on for months, it can regain full use only with care and training. Touch is in danger of becoming a sense enjoyed only in sex. if even there.

If it is true that the sense of touch has diminished, it is likely caused by our insulation from the earth. Consider the earth on a walk outside. The earth is covered by pavement on which you are supposed to walk. But this insulation is not enough. People are supposed to wrap their feet in cloth and then cover this cloth with a piece of leather fastened to some chemical compound. So on the average walk a man or woman is at least three times removed from contact with the earth. Such loss of contact eventually leads to being "out of touch" with the earth. Maybe having everyone walk barefoot on the ground would be the most effective single step to take in solving our ecology problem, the ultimate social sin of being out of touch.

Consider what you were taught not to touch. You were told not to experience rain because you might catch a cold; you were told not to touch your playmates while growing up, unless as a boy you fought back, in which case touching was heroic. You were told that touching food is bad manners. Even the "Don't touch" signs in museums and stores are reminders that our culture does not value touch. As a baby everyone knew that you needed to be cuddled. But what they might not know is that now as a teenager you still have a need to be cuddled, held and touched. Even adults need to be cuddled, especially big, tough men. But sexual contact is the only culturally acceptable way to take care of this need, and "hands off" is still the prevailing policy.

Hearing and Sight

Everyone knows about eyelids, but most people refuse to admit they also have ear lids. Ear lids enable people to select, from the thousands of sounds that come at them, only the ones that they want to hear. Just like the Wild Child, they hear only what they have learned they should hear, and they do this without being aware that the selection process takes place. For example, in school many cases of students "not hearing" the teacher (especially in giving a homework assignment) are actually cases of selective screening out of what the teacher is saying. Unconsciously the person actually decides not to hear because he doesn't want to hear. He probably will not even admit that he didn't hear on purpose, but most of the time this is the case.

We live in a society that has a visual bias, a culture in which "seeing is believing," in which knowledge is identified as in*sight,* in which "I see" indicates understanding, in which thinking is *reflecting* rather than *echoing,* and generally a society in which the sense of hearing plays a minor role compared to that of sight. Perhaps more people have defective hearing than have defective sight, but the number of hearing aids is not at all comparable to the number of eyeglasses.

For primitive man, "hearing is believing." For tribal man, drums still beat louder than the TV, but for twentieth-century man the eye reigns supreme over the ear "Show me, son."

Listening is to hearing what observation is to sight. Hearing and seeing are purely physical, mechanical body processes, but listening and observing are products of training and are psychological processes. Hearing and seeing can be improved only by mechanical devices such as glasses and hearing aids, but observing and listening can be vastly improved by education, although there are few if any classes in school designed specifically to develop your powers to listen or observe. Schools have classes which teach people how to talk, but with all that talking going on, it is strange that not many people are very good listeners.

An observant person is one who can still see and hear the beauty around him, one who sees and appreciates, one who detects meaning where others notice only objects and sounds.

Taste

You've heard of drug addicts, but have you heard of the 200,000,000 Americans who are strung out on chemicals? These Americans (about 95% of the total population, including yourself) daily pop quantities of substances such as monosodium glutamate, calcium phosphate, BHA and BHT, propyl galate, and methyl polysilicone. And, just like many drug users, they refuse to admit that they take these substances or that they really have any permanent effect on them. These substances are just a few of the hundreds of chemicals (many actually poisons) added to food to improve appearances, last longer on the shelf and perhaps even boost profits. Such additives often diminish the natural taste of the food and gradually accustom their users to increasing degrees of tastelessness.

Taste is an important sense. We even use expressions like "good taste" or "tasteless" to indicate our approval or disapproval of fashions or behavior. Imagine being one of the increasing number of Americans suffering from a loss of the sense of taste. Enough cases of the loss of taste have been reported to cause endocrinologists to consider the loss a new disease. Nobody has died yet of this newly discovered disease (known technically as idiopathic hypogeusia), but it has caused suffering.

One fifty-three year old patient was a pizza chef who became so nauseated with the taste and smell of the food he worked with that he had to quit his job. He reported: "Everything seemed rotten, like decaying garbage." In New York a man drank some clam chowder that was so hot it caused his esophagus to close. An operation was performed and a plastic tube inserted into his stomach so that he could receive nourishment. He did feed himself, but still remained undernourished, underweight, and almost constantly hungry. Finally doctors decided that the missing sense was taste, and a system was devised that allowed him to taste his food. From that time on his appetite was healthy and his growth normal. Many who have lost the sense of taste actually experience a general loss of taste for living.

Some Experiments To Help Combat Non-sense

What we detect of the world "out there" comes to us through the senses. If the senses are blocked or numbed, the world appears uninteresting, boring, lifeless. Since formal training in sense education is rarely offered, self-education is the most practical solution. If you take seriously the enjoyable process of developing the potential of your senses, you will discover new worlds and find life more sense-able.

Some of the experiments which follow deal with one sense, while others treat a combination of the senses. Try them as experiments from which you can increase your self-knowledge. Don't try them in the spirit of exercises or homework; enjoy them and see what you learn if you experiment. Over a long period of time you should notice some increase in your sensual awareness.

Smell

Next time you smell a bad odor, stop and think back to your initial experience with that smell. Try to find out why you label the smell bad.

Keep your nose open and describe school in terms of the smells. Try the same thing at your home. Occasionally stop and be aware of what you smell, especially when you change your environment (moving from one room to another, riding in a car, walking).

When you're alone, notice smells more and let your mind wander freely wherever the smells leads. Smells have a power to evoke memories that go far beyond your normal power of recall.

Smell some things in stores. A whiff is still free.

Try to recall the most memorable smell experience of your life.

With a friend, explore the smells in your kitchen. One person presents smells to the other who is blindfolded. Either try to identify the smells, or, even better, say what experience or feeling or past event they recall for you.

Smell food before you eat it.

Touch

When you stretch or relax, imitate a cat. Luxuriate in the experience.

Close your eyes and feel some things that are part of your daily life.

Eat with your hands.

Climb a tree.

Avoid chairs for one (day, week, hour) and learn to sit comfortably on the floor.

How do you feel touching other people and being touched by them? Comfortable? Uncomfortable?

Enjoy touching things. Imitate a baby.

Describe a school or house by touch. Develop a vocabulary all your own to describe how you feel things.

Relax and get in touch with the inside of your body where only you can touch. Like the fictional scientist in *Fantastic Voyage,* close your eyes and make yourself microscopically small. Take a trip through your body.

Decide the kind of touch sensation most objects in school provide.

Hearing

Listen right now. What do you hear? Keep perfectly still and keep listening. What can you hear that you never noticed before? Occasionally stop and listen for the tiny sounds that normally go unheard.

If your eyes are closed, sounds are most noticeable. If your ears are closed, sights become more important. Test this theory.

Take a walk and be especially aware of sounds. Listen to how people sound when they walk.

Listen to someone talk without listening to the content of the words. In other words, listen to how that person sounds rather than to what is being said.

Listen to some music and follow one instrument through the entire song. Switch instruments. Listen to music without doing anything else for one hour.

Sensory Mix

Eat an orange, using all your senses to their utmost. Try listening and touching experiments before you fall asleep.

Take a shower or bath and give full attention to your senses.

At least once a day try an awareness experiment.

Make up your own experiments.

5.
Boredom:
The Great
American Epidemic

The hardened arteries, baldness and wrinkled skin were clearly visible when Richard Gallant died in 1967. Such a death could have marked the end of a long and rich life, but this passing was a tragedy. Ricky Gallant was only eleven years old.

Ricky's rare disease, progeria, compressed seventy years of biological change into a brief eleven. For him, change came too fast. He stands as a tragic warning beacon of the dangers of too much change too fast. Author Alvin Toffler has coined the phrase "Future Shock" to describe the problem of overchange.

Many people seem convinced that things are changing too fast for their own good. They want shock absorbers to cushion them against change. For them change is a frightening event to be avoided. Yet even a casual observer knows that this is not what they really mean. They welcome some changes, yet fear others. What they mean when they say "Things are changing too fast" is really "I don't like the changes going on." If they are granted a raise in salary, if their man is elected president, if the city decides to drop taxation, there is no cry about too much change. So for many it has become fashionable to talk about future shock when they mean a fear of forces beyond their control.

On the other hand, there are those, mostly young people, for whom things don't change fast enough. They are perhaps immunized against the disease of Future Shock, but are highly susceptible to another disease—

boredom. Boredom is the perceived lack of change in the environment. Perceived here means that it really matters little how much change is actually taking place; if the person believes that there is no change, then he is bored.

What is "perceived" must come through the senses. We can gain an understanding of boredom by an experiment which would place a person in a situation where he is unable to perceive much of anything, in a situation where nothing changes.

As long ago as 1954 experiments were being conducted to see what happens when the senses are deprived completely of any input. Twenty-two college men wearing gloves and black-out goggles were placed in a soundproof room. They reclined, resting their heads on foam rubber pillows. The scientists wanted to find out what effects the reduced sense input would have on the men. At first they were restless and unable to sleep. They became emotionally upset and often supplied their own fantasy experiences through hallucinations. Finally a number of the men experienced "blank spaces," a sort of temporary amnesia in which they could not recall what had happened.

What this and many other experiments in sense deprivation have revealed is that in the absence of external sense stimulation people turn more to internal stimulation—fantasies, imagination, thoughts. This explains why people in the desert, where there is little change to attract the senses, see what are called mirages. They compensate for the lack of stimuli by creating their own sights and visions. Blocking the sense of sight, darkening a room, and creating quiet is the most common example of sense deprivation. This leads to sleep in which the mind takes over completely to create a fantastic and almost continual world of dreams. Daydreams are a compensation for the lack of interesting things to listen to or see; they are escapes from boredom.

The ultimate sense deprivation is death. Its relation to boredom can be seen in the common expression "bored to death." Utter boredom puts the person in touch with the deadness within himself, with the complete lack of change and stimuli.

The reaction of the subjects in the experiment is similar to what we do every day. If our senses are under-stimulated, we invent in our minds pictures and sounds. In a dark room or when out on a dark night we tend to be more frightened because one of our senses is disabled and therefore our ears pick up more sounds that we never noticed in the daytime and our imaginations become more active. Ghosts and muggers cause more fear in the darkness of the imagination than in reality. We even cover our ears or eyes sometimes when we want to concentrate on some mental task like a test or to search for some fact buried deep in the memory.

What we learn from experiments in sense deprivation is that in general when one sense is deprived, stopped up or missing, the body somehow compensates. If a sense is permanently blocked, the compensation is likewise permanent. Blind people tend to have a more highly developed sense of hearing than people who can see, and the deaf often develop amazing powers of visual perception.

So what does this all have to do with the dis-ease of boredom? It shows that boredom is not natural in a normally functioning human being. The natural tendency is to compensate and create an interesting world. The kid in the fifth grade who throws a spitball during a boring class and the shipwreck survivor who sees ghost ships on the horizon are both acting naturally. They are creating their own points of interest where none exist; they are dealing with boredom. Both are extremely effective although neither, unfortunately, does the person any good.

Boredom exists when a person is blocked (or blocks himself which is far more common) from experiencing interesting stimuli in his environment.

Take a few minutes right now to make a list of the times or situations in which you are most likely to become bored.

Now look over your list and try to find what all the situations have in common for you. Is there sense deprivation? Is your presence in the situation forced rather than by choice? How do you cope with boredom? If you allow yourself to simply be bored, what is stopping you from dealing with the boredom? Can the situation be changed by your action? Can your attitude be changed? Spend some time right now thinking over the answer to these questions. They are an essential part of this chapter. If you don't wrestle with the questions, you might find this chapter boring. If you do, you might find that your boredom tells you something about yourself.

Looking again at your list of boring things, you will probably find that some or all of the situations on the list have great interest for other people. For example, I find watching some TV shows a bore, while millions of other people find them thoroughly enjoyable. My conclusion is that it is not the situations on the list that are boring, but something in each person that causes him to consider them boring.

Nothing in itself is boring. Boredom is in the eye

of the beholder. When you say "That's a bore" you are saying more about yourself than about whatever it is that's a bore. Catch yourself making that statement sometime and try to find what it says about you. Do the same with the list of boring situations. Is it possible to avoid being bored in any situation?

There's a difference between saying, for example, "He's a boring teacher" and "In his class I'm bored." In the first statement the "blame" is placed on the teacher, thus freeing the student from responsibility, and he will likely remain bored. In the second statement the student might realize that he is boring himself or at least allowing himself to be bored by the teacher. If he recognized that he has some responsibility, some freedom in the situation, he might be able to do something about it.

The impish fifth grade spitball thrower knew that he could change his boring situation into an interesting (even daring, exciting) one, although his solution hardly helped his education or anyone else in the room. Gang fights, drag races, drug experiments, spouse swapping, TV addiction, and maybe even suicide all are often attempted responses to boredom.

One problem with all these responses is that they are escapes rather than solutions. A person who turns to any one of these excitements (or even to more respectable ones like sports, travel, parties, and hobbies) as an escape from boredom fails to deal with the boring situation which makes him want to escape in the first place. Escapes eventually become boring themselves, and finally there is nowhere left to escape and tragedy results. The basic problem is that the person never felt he could deal with the boring situation by a means other than replacing 9 to 5 boredom with 8 to 1 daring.

Dealing honestly with boredom and its causes is a challenge more often than not rejected.

A person who honestly confronts his own boredom might discover that he is using boredom as a weapon. For example, let's say that your parents want to spend a summer vacation in a resort town on a Wisconsin lake. You want to stay home and enjoy your friends, your usual haunts, and summer activities. In spite of your protest you wind up at the lake with your parents. You act totally bored with the whole vacation; you mope around, lie on the bed half the day, read the same mystery three times, and flare into anger at the slightest provocation.

You loudly claim the entire set-up a "big bore" and act accordingly. What you really are doing, even though you might not admit it immediately, is punishing your parents for making you come on the vacation instead of letting you stay at home. Your boredom is an effort to get back at your parents and prove you were right and shouldn't have been forced to come on the trip.

Looking honestly at the situation, you can see that the new environment probably offers many new stimuli to explore, new friends to meet and new activities to try. Many teens see very clearly the "ruts" their parents are caught in, but they do not realize that they themselves have their own ruts that they like to stay in and do not want to be forced out of. What the teen in our example is saying is, "If you're not going to let me stay in my ruts, I'm going to make things miserable for you." So his sulking boredom is a weapon, freely chosen by him, to punish his parents.

Another insight that might be gained by the person who confronts his boredom is that he feels pressured or under control from outside forces that in reality don't have the power to control him. This is especially true of people who view themselves as not free because of their parents or school or "society" rather than because of themselves.

Boring situations (check your own list) are often ones in which we are there because we feel we *should be,* not because we feel we *want to.*

Consider the difference between the feeling of doing something because you *want to* and doing the same thing because you *should.* Take going to sleep, for example. If you are tired and want to go to bed, it's easy; you simply do what you want. But if your younger brothers and sisters have to go to bed at a certain time because they *should,* then sleep is eight times as difficult. Or take getting up in the morning. Feel the difference between those mornings when you awake simply because you *should* and those exciting mornings when you can't wait for the day to start.

People whose actions are constantly motivated by "should" are easy victims for continual boredom, neurosis and even "nervous breakdowns." Such people eventually lose touch with what they want, and life becomes a constant struggle to follow every "should" learned from parents and school. One person defined a neurotic as "full of should."

There is a natural conflict inside people between the voice that says "This is what you should do" (often called conscience) and the voice that says "This is what I want to do." The healthy person is one who doesn't have this conflict, and such people are rare. What they want to do and what they feel they should do merge into one, and they seem to almost instinctively make choices that contribute to their happiness. Such a healthy person might be doing exactly the same things that his neighbor does, yet the neighbor is a neurotic wreck. They both go to church, play golf, work at an office, have a pet dog, are married and share basically the same moral standards. Yet one is enjoying life and the other finds living a burden. The difference is that the healthy person is doing what he does out of "want," while the other is doing what he does out of "should," to keep his image, to keep up with the neighbors, to be just like everyone else, etc.

It might sound daring to say, but, very simply, the healthy person is one who consistently does what he wants. He might be a rebel non-conformist or he might act just like you or me, but no matter what he does, it is because he wants to.

If you know how it feels to act on a "should" motivation, observe yourself. The next time you catch yourself doing something simply because you feel you "should," try to figure out where that "should" comes from. Parents? School? Your need for acceptance or conformity? Friends? Then examine to see what you want to do. Ask yourself: "What am I doing to prevent myself from doing what I want to?" Carry on a conversation with those two parts of yourself, the one that says "should" and the one that says "want." See what they have to say to each other. See if you can't change some "shoulds" into "wants."

For example, if you baby-sit simply because you feel you "should," see if you can't find some reason that would make you want to baby-sit. If you succeed, there would be less boredom while baby-sitting, less struggle to do it, and less likelihood that you will spend part of the day dreading baby-sitting.

Some may fear that if people acted according to

what they wanted, everyone would turn out selfish, inconsiderate, cruel, lazy, sloppy, or murderous. But since people don't normally "want" to be any of these things, such a situation is less likely to happen than if people frustrate themselves with dozens of "shoulds."

Many of the "shoulds" you have are very good ones, but if they remain on the level of a "should" they are never really made a part of your personality. There are many fifty year olds who still play-act the role of the obedient child doing what he should, even though the parents are long dead and the "shoulds" now irrelevant. In fact many adults have never really matured. They simply play the roles of adults; they act the way they believe grown-ups "should." In so doing they trap themselves in a life they don't want and which defies escape.

Parents usually transmit to their children the "shoulds" they picked up from their parents, some of which are valid and some are not. The dangerous aspect of examining your "shoulds" is that as a teen you might find some "shoulds" that your parents impose on you that you don't agree with or understand. The dishonest approach is to conform to the "shoulds" when your parents are watching but to ignore them when away from them. The honest approach is to let them know how you feel.

Doing what you want sounds revolutionary, almost sinful, yet it is as natural as the birth of a baby or the growth of a plant. What would happen if people were in touch with what they really wanted? I find it hard to believe that what people really want is to spend hours griping about the boss, kids and taxes and to spend two hundred hours a year traveling to and from work. Are people who save for a better color TV and a newly paved driveway for a slightly restyled car doing what they want? Do they really want to spend an average of two to five hours a day mindlessly in front of a television and eat food that has been processed so thoroughly that it is tasteless? People who play roles finally lose touch with what they really want; their desires become buried in daydreams and fantasies that they never live out.

A Gallup poll turned up a frightening statistic two years ago that has probably not changed much since. Fifty-one percent of all Americans were willing to admit to the polltakers that their lives were mostly dull and routine. And how many are there who refuse to admit even to themselves that they are afflicted with the epidemic of boredom?

6.
This Thing Called Love

Notes on Ancient Love Potions

In India a girl who wanted a certain man prepared betel nuts or tobacco and hid them in his pouch.

Among the Creoles, roast hummingbird hearts were ground into a powder and sprinkled on the beloved in an attempt to insure the return of love.

Some Australian tribes used testicles of kangaroos and some American Indians used beaver testicles to help capture love.

Arunta women placed necklaces of their hair around the necks of the men they wanted to "catch."

Notes from Television Ads

Sexy hair comes naturally when you use Groom and Clean.

With Certs, if she kissed you once, she'll kiss you again.

Boy: Hi! I think I'm in love.
Friend: Did you talk to her?
Boy: Yeah, but she turned off like I had bad breath.
Friend: How about a little of that . . . ?
Boy: If I use Listerine every day, I get the girl, right?
Friend: Unless she gets you first.

In Newfoundland those who believed in charms pricked an apple full of holes and carried the apple under their left arm for a while and then gave it to their beloved.

No more ignored, now I'm adored, since I switched to Ultra Brite! Ultra Brite toothpaste gives your mouth sex appeal.

From beaver testicles to toothpaste, humans have searched for magical substances that would result in the user being loved. The custom of exchanging class rings or of buying an engagement and wedding ring is related to the magic charms and bracelets used by primitive peoples. Today the advertising agency has replaced the tribal medicine man, but the message is the same. If you want to be loved, use the right products, say the right words, and wear the right "charms." The only difference is that primitive people managed without television and brand names.

Countless attempts have been made to describe what love is. An ancient myth found in several religions tells of a time when mankind existed in an androgynous form—meaning that each individual was both male and female. According to the myth, man committed some mysterious crime and in punishment the gods split people into two. Ever since these two halves of this once united creature have been seeking each other out with varying degrees of success. According to this myth, the search for man's lost wholeness is what we call love. In some cultures love is regarded as a rare form of insanity; others have no word for love except as another way of describing sexual desire. Still other societies have no word at all in their language for love.

One common modern belief about love is that it happens naturally like the first cry of a baby. In reality love is an attitude that must be learned; it is never "fallen" into. Learning to love might be the most crucial educational experience a person goes through and is usually done without help from school and often in spite of parents. It is a skill rarely learned easily and one that is desperately needed.

How much of a need is love? The absence of love can kill. Some doctors say that children who lack love develop small and fragile bones (this does not mean that everyone with small and fragile bones grew up without love). Educators often realize that the amount of love in a family deeply affects the ability of children to do well in school. Perhaps the absence of love can even prove fatal.

War sometimes makes studies possible that would otherwise be inhuman to conduct. Such was the case in World War II where bombing raids on England caused many homes to be destroyed and fathers to be separated from mothers and children. Institutions that were half hospital and half orphanage were set up to take care of the homeless. One study after the war took a close look at 240 children who were in such an institution for a year or more from their birth. About half were cared for by their mothers, while the other half were motherless and so were cared for by the staff in the ratio of one nurse for every ten babies. Of the babies who had their mothers present, none died and all seemed normal when examined by the scientists. The others who were cared for by the nurses were all equally well fed and attended to while at the institution, yet well over one-third of them had died. With only a few exceptions, the survivors in the second group were "human wrecks who behaved in the manner of overly excited or half dead idiots." And yet both groups had their physical needs well satisfied. The only factor that could account for the dramatic difference was that the babies with their mothers received the attention that only love can motivate, especially frequent cuddling and physical handling.

So to say that loving parents are a "need" is no mere figure of speech but a very real fact. A parent's love assures the child that he is "O.K."—good and valuable in himself and therefore worthy of love. This "I'm O.K." message is one that a loved child learns probably even before he can talk. He learns it deep inside, non-verbally, and he learns so well that he never forgets. The first step in learning to love is to be loved.

There is no better way to learn to love than to live in a loving family for about twenty years. Yet there are many people who have never lived in an atmosphere of love but have still taught themselves how to love. They learned loving by going out to others and taking risks, by showing trust instead of mistrust and warmth instead of detachment. They found the learning to be painful and difficult but rewarding.

Love is like an art that can be learned. Love is not something one is *in;* rather it is what one does. Love is not the sublime passion or the answer to all mankind's ills. It is the active concern for the life and growth of another person or persons. Someone has suggested that since the word love is used so much, even to refer to gasoline, hamburgers and abstract ideas, it should be banned for ten years from our vocabulary.

An artist does not create art by waiting around for the right picture to appear; he works hard and paints consistently. One does not learn the art of love by waiting for the right person either. Lovers, like artists, learn to love by loving. They don't ask, "Why doesn't anyone love me?" Instead they love others and thereby make themselves lovable. The lovable person is simply one who loves, not one who has a certain figure, a pretty face or an abundance of wealth. A lover, in the deepest sense of the word, is one who has concerned himself with "How I can love others" rather than with "How I can appear more lovable."

If love is a slowly learned art, then what is that passionate experience called "falling in love"? What about feeling like you're walking on a cloud, anxious to swim the widest river to prove your love and thinking of the person you love three times every two minutes? Isn't this true love? No. But whatever it is, these feelings are some of the most powerful a person can experience during a lifetime. Adults who say it's *only* infatuation probably don't remember how powerful and even overwhelming it is. The labels "infatuation" or "puppy love" don't do justice to these feelings. "Romantic Love" is perhaps the most apt term to classify this state of mad, passionate, all-consuming "love."

It is the nature of Romantic Love that it doesn't last a lifetime. If it did, one or both of the lovers would probably be a basket case before their third anniversary together. Romantic Love is powerful, valuable, and crucial but it is not a prelude to marriage. In fact Romantic Love is more likely to lead to divorce than to mature and lasting love. In a sense the divorce rate in this country is so high because people marry out of Romantic Love. Romantic Love should be enjoyed and suffered through while free of pressure to get married. It is possible that Romantic Love can lead to mature love, but one does not automatically follow the other.

When talking about Romantic Love people will say, "Love is blind." "You're the blind ones," say the lovers. People look at Fritz and Patsy and see perhaps a couple of typical kids or maybe even one creep and one very likable person. Fritz and Patsy look at each other and little explosions happen and each thinks the other is nearly a god or goddess. Who's blind? The people who see only two kids or the two lovers? Really neither. If John and Mary are in a period of Romantic Love they look into each other and see themselves. The excitement of Romantic Love is really the delight of self-discovery. Romantic Love could be accurately described as a crash course in self-exploration. It is a period of rediscovering feelings and of exploring new feelings and thoughts never before revealed to anyone.

Take Fritz, for example. Part of what he discovers in Patsy are his own hidden desires to be soft and cuddled—desires and feelings which have been hidden in him for many years. If Fritz could think back to himself as a little boy (or observe the same process in his younger brother), he would find that at one time he used to kiss his dad good night and hug his mother every hour or so and very likely kiss lots of other strangers who might be around at his bedtime.

Little Fritz needs this softness and touching. But slowly he learns that a male does not do things like that once he grows up. So the kiss to his father changes to a handshake, and he begins to be more "tough" than cuddly. He might even make ugly faces if his grandpa kisses him and make a big show of wiping off the kiss. The only problem with this learning process is that the need to touch and be touched, to be soft and tender, is still part of Fritz, even though he might vehemently deny their existence. There are a number of other urges that Fritz has learned to ignore as well.

Along comes Patsy or any person who still accepts her need to touch and be touched and to be soft, and Fritz can finally express and satisfy his long denied need to interact with his repressed urges. The same thing happens in reverse to Patsy who has perhaps been taught that being intelligent or tough or agressive is improper.

Romantic Love would probably take place between people of the different sexes even if everyone agreed to remain a virgin for life. The reason for this is that many of the characteristics which we teach boys and girls as not being proper to their sex are ones which our culture permits in the opposite sex. This is why the attraction between sexes is more than mere biology. Each person has within the qualities of both sexes; psychologically each person is both masculine and feminine. But depending on how they are raised, they learn to deny certain parts of themselves.

In most cultures there are some activities, likes, and personality traits which are classified as being "masculine" or "feminine." What is normal "masculine" behavior in one culture might be considered "feminine" in another. Among the Tchambuli of New Guinea, women are expected to be practical and sexually aggressive while the men are passive, artistic and encouraged to gossip and primp. A large part of what you are today has been determined by what our culture expects of you as transmitted through your parents. If you were born in New Guinea as a male, you might today be busy sewing and gossiping while your girl was painting the hut or running the village politics.

The problem with this learning about being "male"

and "female" is that individuals of both sexes learn in the process to be only half-human. Men disown their feminine selves and women disown their masculine selves, but this disowning does not destroy that part of them. Men still have desires to be cuddled, pretty, irrational, giggly, tender and emotional, and women still have the desire to be self-assertive, good in sports, mechanical, rational, cool, practical and tough. But society frowns upon the expression of these tendencies.

Society's roles for men and women are not direct opposites, but they contrast enough to account for much of the attraction between the sexes. Those who assume that this magnetism between the sexes is "natural" should be aware that it is not so in many cultures. Among the classical Greeks homosexual love among men was the most respected kind of love. For a man to fall in love with a woman was unusual. Attraction between sexes is a pattern of behavior which a culture teaches to its members.

Many teens go through a period of Romantic Love for a friend of the same sex. Such "love" is not a sign of a lifetime of homosexuality. It is possible for Romantic Love between persons of the same sex to serve the same need for self-discovery as the more common love between different sexes. The greatest problem in such an experience is the fear of the persons involved that they are not "normal." Realizing that such experiences are very common can help to quiet those fears and doubts.

Romantic Love provides fond memories of time spent together and is one of the most psychologically valuable experiences in growing up, but it is not one step from the altar. Consider what would happen to people who married out of Romantic Love. Invariably the "love" would begin to fade. Since they believe that their strong passions are really mature love, they are led to believe that they no longer love each other. Soon their relationship becomes cold, even irritating; the fact that they agree love has faded often causes them to act in a loveless way toward each other. The great tragedy of Romantic Love is that somehow it has become associated with marriage. The misconception is that marriage will prolong this necessarily temporary state. But Romantic Love is temporary, and so a marriage based on such love often leads to tragedy, although there are enough exceptions to show that human nature can overcome such obstacles. It is no accident that the great love classics of literature, from *Romeo and Juliet* to *Love Story,* have tragic endings.

It is possible that the Romantic Love will be replaced by true love and a genuine desire to live together and raise children. But there is nothing in the process of Romantic Love that magically changes into mature love.

From this viewpoint it follows that if children were raised so that they developed both the masculine and feminine aspects of their personalities, many of the tragic aspects of Romantic Love would disappear. In fact, current trends of unisex and a change in the traditional dating patterns among college students indicate that such a change might already be taking place. There will still be caring and genuine concern of people for each other, but people would not live together solely to fill the holes in their personalities. They would live together not out of psychological need but out of the joy of being together—a much healthier environment for the cultivation of true and mature love.